THE SPIRIT
OF THE
CHINESE
CHARACTER

∎

THE SPIRIT OF THE CHINESE CHARACTER

GIFTS FROM THE HEART

歌調寶生
吳文忠

Barbara Aria with Russell Eng Gon
Calligraphy by Russell Eng Gon

Chronicle Books
San Francisco

A RUNNING HEADS BOOK

Copyright © 1992 by Running Heads Incorporated

THE SPIRIT OF THE CHINESE CHARACTER
was conceived and produced by
Running Heads Incorporated
55 West 21 Street
New York, New York 10010

ISBN 0–8118–0142–X

Library of Congress Cataloging-in-Publication Data
Aria, Barbara.
The spirit of the Chinese character : 40 gifts from the heart /
text by Barbara Aria ; calligraphy by Russell Eng Gon
       p.   cm.
Includes index.
ISBN 0-8118-0142-X
1. Chinese language—Writing.   2. Chinese language—Etymology.
3. Philosophy, Chinese.   I. Gon, Russell Eng.   II. Title.
            PL1171.A76   1992
495.1'11—dc20   91-39744   CIP

Editor: Rose K. Phillips
Designer: Lesley Ehlers
Managing Editor: Jill Hamilton
Production Manager: Peter J. McCulloch

Distributed in Canada by
Raincoast Books
112 East 3rd Avenue
Vancouver, B.C. V5T 1C8

1   3   5   7   9   10   8   6   4   2

Chronicle Books
275 Fifth Street
San Francisco, California 94103

Typeset by Trufont Typographers Inc.
Color Separations by Hong Kong Scanner Craft Company, Ltd.
Printed and bound in Hong Kong by C&C Offset Printing Co., Ltd.

Acknowledgements

We would like to thank the following people for all the
effort they put into making this book happen:
Marta Hallett of Running Heads Incorporated, who
gave us her idea for the book, and Caroline Herter and
Lesley Bruynesteyn of Chronicle Books, who supported
the development of that idea. Our thanks also to the
staff at Running Heads, and in particular to
Rose K. Phillips, our editor. Special thanks to
Lesley Ehlers who did such a wonderful job
of designing this book.

CONTENTS

Introduction

"Words are the voice of the heart; calligraphy is the painting of the heart."

Master Yang

The written character has always had spiritual significance in the culture of China. In its beginnings during the second millennium B.C.—a time on the verge of myth—writing was known only to the priestly class, who in the service of the kings inscribed characters on pieces of shell and bone and, through a process of divination, received omens from the gods as to the correct times of planting, the feasibility of invasion, and other matters of state. In time, this priestly class was transformed into the scholarly literati, the class that produced the major philosophies of China.

The ancients penned characters as a means of spiritual elevation, for it was considered possible to express the essential spirit of the universe through brushwork. In Chinese thought, the act of writing a character is seen as parallel to the universal process of creation, and an embodiment of the principles that govern all life. Just as 'spirit', or 'energy', creates all living things in the universe, so the human spirit creates art. In this system of beliefs, just as the universe was created from primeval chaos in one single stroke, so can it be expressed in one stroke that signifies the whole of nature and humanity.

Likewise, every character derives from the first brush stroke, the one that preceded all others. This mirrors the idea that the universe was created from an original 'oneness'—a central idea in Chinese thought as it developed over the centuries.

This 'oneness'—or *Tao* as the Taoists named it—came out of primeval chaos, and represents a system of order or essential law which governs the entire universe.

From the one came two.

From the two came the ten thousand things of this world, each of which—from the leaf, to the human, to the planets themselves—having come originally from the one, contains within itself the germ of the original, the life principle, as well as its own way of expressing that principle. Each, in other words, is imbued with its own internal law or 'way'. Among people, this law is expressed as human nature, which in classical Chinese thought is believed to be essentially good.

Since everything in the universe is linked together by a shared origin, a shared spirit or 'energy', and each being has its place in the whole, there exists a natural tendency toward harmony. In nature, everything works together perfectly: that is nature's way. Only people have the ability to stray from human nature as it originally expressed itself. The leaf can do nothing but float and be carried, the sheep follows with no thought.

The focus of the Chinese philosophers was on how harmony could be restored and maintained between human life and the life of the universe. Out of this focus came the Confucianist moral philosophy of "human-heartedness" and correctness, and the Taoist philosophy of simplicity and self-purification, both of which helped to shape the spirit of the Chinese character. The philosophy of Confucius, who lived from 551 B.C. to 479

B.C., was adopted as official state teaching by the first century B.C., having absorbed elements of Taoism, which is thought to have been developed by monks during or soon after the lifetime of Confucius.

According to the Confucians, the path to harmony lies in developing certain essential qualities that are innate in human nature—what Confucius called the four constant virtues: compassion or benevolence, righteousness, propriety, and wisdom. These are developed using oneself as a measure of one's conduct toward others—"Do unto others as you would have done unto yourself" is a famous Confucian saying.

In practicing human-heartedness we gradually lose the selfishness that invades the spirit, and in becoming less selfish we cast off the false distinctions we once made between people, and between the world of people and the universe at large. Thus, we perceive the essential unity of the universe. In the process, we improve not only ourselves but also our environment—the world of people—just as the tree, true to its own nature, spreads and gives shade, and in turn influences its environment.

The Taoists, on the other hand, rejected society, seeing seclusion and the serious contemplation of nature as the path to the realization of universal nature. We need only yield, quietly and passively, to our inner law, while stimulating our spiritual understanding of all nature—including the human—through observance of the mountains, the streams, the animals, and their actions.

Shih-t'ao, a famous artist-monk born during the Ming Dynasty (1368 to 1644), presented the action of water as a model for the human spirit. Among water's many qualities, its virtue lies in the fact that it reaches out in rivers and lakes, spreading its benefits. It shows its strength in crashing waves. It is clean and pure in essence, this being its goodness. It flows by its own law, swirling and finding its level with no motive or effort whatsoever. Like water, truly virtuous people simply follow their own true nature and do what they do for its own sake.

Similarly, the art of calligraphy is seen as a matter of letting the true spirit within flow free, without hindrance from the striving that is so uncharacteristic of nature's actions. It is said that the artist Wang Hsi-chih, having once written the best calligraphy of his life, tried to copy it dozens of times yet failed, because he was trying.

It is the spirit that moves the brush, creating that rhythmic vitality of line that is a primary and essential quality in the art of calligraphy. The brush moving along, guided by the heart, is its ch'i,—its spirit or 'energy'.

The Spirit of the Chinese Character introduces forty characters depicting words, or concepts, connected with the human spirit. Some of these concepts translate only approximately into English. The word normally translated as 'heart', for instance—a word that forms the basis of many characters in this book—really means both the heart itself, the seat of the emotions, and also the mind, for the 'heart' governs all human thought and action. And, there exist at least five Chinese words for our 'happiness', each with a different shade of meaning.

The written language of China is essentially a picture language. Originally, primitive drawings, called "pictograms," were used to denote concrete ideas—sun and moon, animals and plants, man, woman and child, and so on. As time went by, these drawings were stylized. Where relevant, the evolution of the characters from their original form is shown in this book.

With the increasing complexity and sophistication of Chinese civilization, and the gradual transformation of the priestly class into the literati, the need arose for characters that could express not just physical things, but emotional and intellectual concepts too—the language of the spirit. How could these abstractions be signified through pictures?

The answer lay in metaphor. Through combinations of images, called "ideograms," any number of ideas can be evoked. The character for 'good', for example, is formed by combining the pictograms for 'woman' and 'child'. This tells us that the essence of human 'goodness' is epitomized by a mother's selfless and intuitive nurturing of her child.

Since the human and natural worlds mirror each other, many of the characters in this book express their meaning through analogy with nature, and above all with water, in which so many qualities of the spirit can be perceived—as the monk Shih-t'ao so aptly demonstrated. Some pictograms, like 'water', have an abbreviated form, called a 'radical,' which is used in combination with other characters.

Every Chinese character has its own way of being formed, known as its "stroke order." For those who want to heighten their appreciation of the characters in this book by writing them, the stroke order for each is presented. It is considered crucial to follow this sequence in writing characters, since it represents universal order and the harmonious movement visible in nature. A character whose strokes are made in the wrong sequence is said to look unnatural and discordant.

There are seven kinds of stroke, known as the "seven mysteries." Each requires a particular movement of the hand and arm. Chinese children practice these strokes diligently—horizontal and vertical strokes, sweeping right and left strokes, dots, hooks, and diagonal strokes. The person who has mastered all of these is able to write the character for 'eternity', whose seven strokes represent each of the seven mysteries.

Spirit   Shen

According to Chinese mythology, when we are born and enter the world of light we receive the part of our soul which, at death, ascends to heaven and becomes a *shen* or active 'spirit'. In ancient days special signs, believed to have been made by ancestral spirits, were divined to determine decisions of state. Thus *shen*, the character, combines 'to divine' and 'sign', or 'to give orders'.

The word *shen* is paired with others to produce terms relating to 'spirit' as it is manifested in our own life. *Shen-ch'ing*, literally 'spirit-condition', gives us our 'facial expression'; *shen-ch'i*, a 'forced spirit', means 'conceited'.

The Way   Tao

Originally, *tao* meant simply a 'course of action', perhaps a military one: The character combines 'foot' or 'to follow', with 'the leader'—a 'head' topped with the two plumes that were used in ancient days to signify the rank of general.

To Confucius *tao* became the 'way' of moral rectitude—the way we do what we do. It was Lao-tzu who interpreted *Tao* as the law, or truth of the universe, the oneness from which sprang the ten thousand things, each of which contains within it the law or *tao* of its own being. In Taoism, to see not only things but the *tao* of things, is to follow the *Tao*.

Virtue   Te

Lao-tzu said, "Not to part from the invari-
able *te* is to return to the state of infancy." In
Taoism, *te* is essential virtue—an inborn
quality, and the true, original nature of hu-
mankind. The infant still retains this virtuous
inner self, as does the person who has never
left its path.

Therefore, the character for *te*—a sim-
plified 'foot', combined on the right with the
modified character for 'true', above 'heart'—
tells us: Follow the path of the true heart.

Te also means 'power', for the virtuous
person thereby becomes spiritually powerful.
The original name for Taoism is *Tao-te Chia*,
"the School of the Way and Its Power."

20

Tranquility   An

The character for 'tranquility' is rooted in the ancient Chinese tradition of male dominance. A 'woman' under a man's 'roof' indicates that all is as it should be.

But *an* has a richer meaning, reflecting the parallel between microcosm and macrocosm. Just as a harmonious relationship between man and woman brings tranquility to the heart, peace comes when universal energies are in harmony—the forceful, creative energy of heaven above, and the gentle, receptive energy of the earth below.

Tranquility: when our world is in order.

Peace   P'ing

A pictogrammatic 'shield' or 'bamboo stem' is balanced on each side by a single tongue of 'fire', producing *p'ing*.

The character for 'peace' illustrates a vital principle in classical Chinese thought—the principle of balance between opposing forces. When there is equilibrium among humans, then nature and the heavens are balanced, and peace prevails.

The character can also be interpreted to represent a balance of power: Equal shields on either side lead to peace.

Truth   Fu

Many Chinese characters are based on images from nature, making striking, figurative
comparisons between phenomena in the natural world and certain qualities inherent in
human life.

   The character for 'truth' shows a pictogrammatic 'bird's foot' over its 'young'. Just as
the bird broods the egg, within which is concealed the germ of life, essential truth, which
is concealed, can be discovered by contem-
plating the universal nature of life.

Unity   Hsieh

The fact that a huge and varied country like China has existed as a powerful civilization for over two thousand years is due in part to the importance placed on the concept of unity, or *hsieh*—a concept of social organization mirroring the unified order of the universe.

Initially, it was the written language itself that unified the country, and the character for 'unity' acknowledges the benefits. The character denoting 'three' (basically, any number above two) combines with 'ten', meaning 'complete' or 'pulled together' (from ten fingers, a complete count), and with the character for 'strength' or 'power': United we stand.

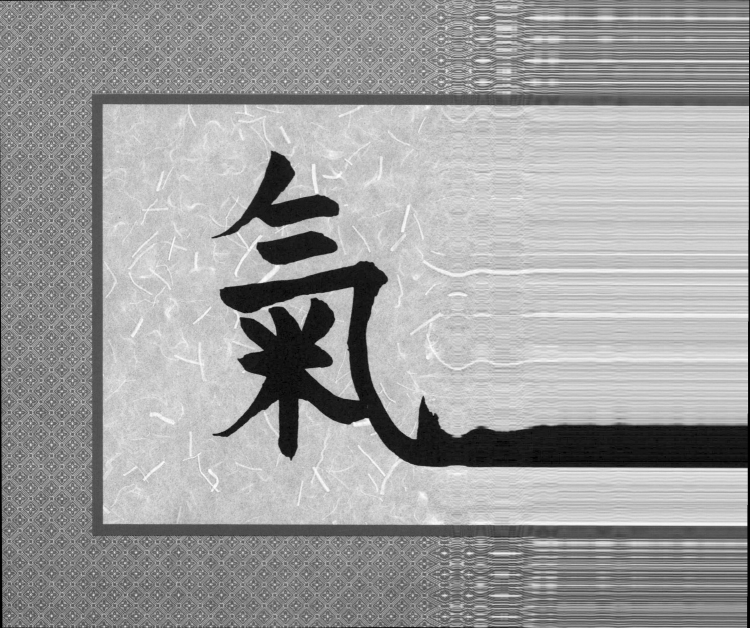

Truth   Fu

Many Chinese characters are based on images from nature, making striking, figurative
comparisons between phenomena in the natural world and certain qualities inherent in
human life.

The character for 'truth' shows a pictogrammatic 'bird's foot' over its 'young'. Just as
the bird broods the egg, within which is concealed the germ of life, essential truth, which
is concealed, can be discovered by contem-
plating the universal nature of life.

27

Unity   Hsieh

The fact that a huge and varied country like China has existed as a powerful civilization for over two thousand years is due in part to the importance placed on the concept of unity, or *hsieh*—a concept of social organization mirroring the unified order of the universe.

Initially, it was the written language itself that unified the country, and the character for 'unity' acknowledges the benefits. The character denoting 'three' (basically, any number above two) combines with 'ten', meaning 'complete' or 'pulled together' (from ten fingers, a complete count), and with the character for 'strength' or 'power': United we stand.

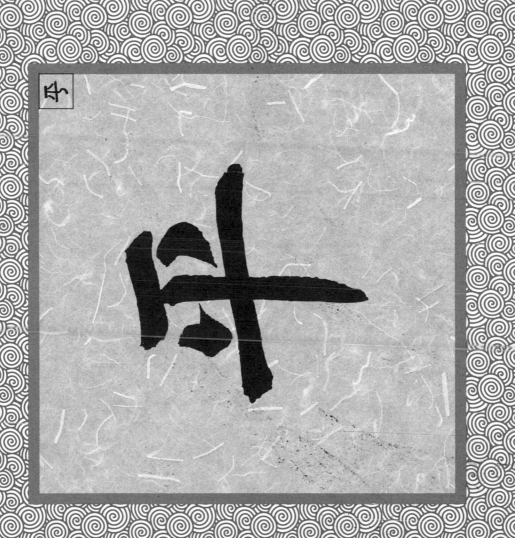

Energy   Ch'i

No precise equivalent exists in the English language for *ch'i*, the spiritual 'energy' or, literally, 'vapor' that forms all matter, including human life. The character is an ideogram composed of 'breath' above the pictogram for 'uncooked rice'. By placing the 'rice' character beneath the horizontal base of the upper character, or 'earth line', the idea of 'deep', or 'universal', is evoked.

   Ch'i, then, is the universal breath or energy that gives us our material existence, and is reflected in our appearance or *ch'i-ch'ing* ('energy-image'). Some people are endowed at birth with an impure energy, and their true nature is, according to the sage Chu-hsi, hidden like a pearl in muddy water.

Eternity Yung

Just as the sun never ceases to rise and set, or the moon to progress through its cycles, so water never ceases to flow, down from the mountains, into the ocean where it foams and ripples, vaporizes and condenses, and again pours down as rain into mountain streams.

This simple and poetic character for eternity—formed around the image of running 'water', with the two horizontal strokes denoting 'foam and ripples'—contains the seven fundamental strokes in calligraphy, from which every character in the Chinese language can be made.

Clarity   Ch'ing

Ch'ing means 'clear', 'lucid', and 'pure'. The character is a simple ideogram composed of two elements: 'water', represented by the three 'drops' of the water radical (an abbreviated form of 'water'), and 'the color of nature'.

"Keep clear the originally clear character," said Confucius. When water has clarity you see in it the color that nature gave it, just as the essential humaneness that nature gave us shines through when our energy is pure, like a pearl through clear water.

This was the title chosen by China's last imperial dynasty in 1644, which called itself the Ch'ing Dynasty.

Enlightenment   Ming

The dynasty that presided over China's age of
enlightenment called itself Ming—'bright' or
'enlightened'. It seems natural and fitting that
the character describing an understanding
that all things are one should itself be su-
premely simple. *Ming* is composed of two
ancient pictograms in their modern, stylized
form: 'sun', *jih*, and 'moon', *yüeh*. *Jih* was
originally represented by a round, primitive
sun drawing, *yüeh* by a crescent moon.

Together they light the world.

Profundity   Hung

Like 'clarity', the character for 'profundity' of
thought and understanding is formed around
the three 'drops' of the water radical. Combined, on the right, with the character denoting 'collective effort', and 'all' or 'the whole',
hung suggests the immense depth of water.

People who seek the profundity of deep
water do not skim the surface in their percep-
tions, but strive for an understanding of the
whole universe in its essential unity.

丶
冫
氵
氵一
氵十
氵丗
洪
洪
洪

Gentleness   Shun

A 'leaf' in a 'stream'—both ancient picto-grammatic images from nature—denotes the idea of 'gentleness' and 'ease', or *shun*. The leaf floats along in the running stream without striving or resistance, letting the motion of the water influence its course and destiny.

This character epitomizes the ideal of gentleness in Chinese culture. 'Gentle' is almost synonymous with 'favorable', and the two words are occasionally used interchangeably, as in the saying "May favorable *[shun]* winds fill your sail."

40

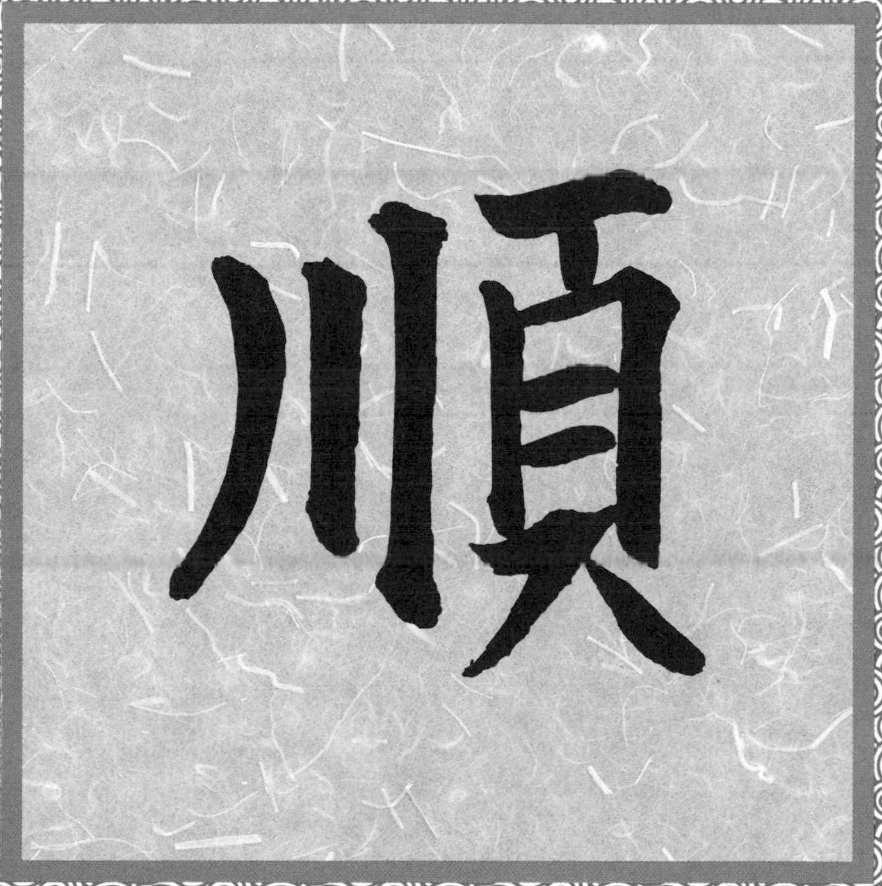
順

Beauty   Mei

The character for *mei* combines two pictograms to express the Chinese ideal of 'beauty'.

Above is the character for 'sheep', showing the face and horns of the animal traditionally seen by the Chinese as a model of gentleness and passivity: the inner beauty implied by *mei*. Sheep have no will, no striving. They follow their natures and live in harmony with one another. Below 'sheep' is the pictogram denoting 'big' or 'adult'—a 'person' with arms outstretched.

Beauty: the docility of a sheep as displayed by an adult.

43

Righteousness 義

Confucianism insists on 'righteousness', one of the four inborn virtues which, if cultivated, can purify our spiritual energy. The character for *I* is built around the image of the selfless and docile 'sheep', above the character for 'I' or 'me', composed of a 'hand' and a 'spear'.

The great Confucianist philosopher Mencius (c. 371 B.C. to 289 B.C.) defined *I* as doing what we should as "citizens of the universe," while Confucius stressed doing what we should purely for its own sake, without desire for material or spiritual gain. Perhaps these definitions help to explain the character: *I* is a selfless condition of 'oughtness', which inevitably cultivates the self.

Benevolence   Jên

Jên, or benevolence, the first of the four virtues considered by Confucius to be innate in
humans, can also be translated as 'kindness' or
'humanity'. The ideas are inseparable. It is
our humanity that prompts us to do good unto
others, as we would have done unto ourselves.

This ideogram combines the radical for
'human being' (also pronounced *jên*), showing
the legs and trunk of a person, with the pair of
horizontal strokes that denotes 'two'.

Benevolence: the essential kindness that
one person shows to another.

Grace

En

A pictogrammatic image of the 'heart' (which in its ancient form showed the chambers and aorta) forms the basis of many Chinese characters connected with the spirit, including *en*, or 'grace'. In Chinese, 'heart' means the higher human feelings and attributes, including the mind and moral character.

In the character for 'grace', the 'heart', below, combines with *yin*, an ancient pictogram of a person 'resting upon' a square mat. Later, *yin* came to mean also 'rely upon' (and today is used for 'because'). The person who relies on his heart achieves grace.

Compassion   Tz'u

It is natural for us to want to help those in need, especially the young and helpless. This is why many Confucians believed in the essential goodness of human nature. If we see a child fall into a well, for instance, we automatically try to save the child.

Compassionate kindness—epitomized best of all, perhaps, by the quality of a mother's love for her children—is evoked in an early version of the character by the image of a 'son' and 'daughter' cradled over a 'heart'. Today, in a universalization of the concept, the children are represented by the light strokes of tender young 'grass'.

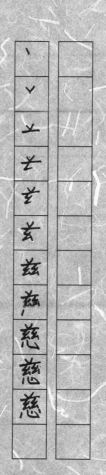

Forgiveness   Shu

"Forgiveness is the action of the heart" is a
traditional Chinese saying.

In the character for *shu*, 'forgiveness', the
'heart' pictogram is complemented by the
character for 'like' or 'equal to', which is in
turn made up of a pictogrammatic 'woman'
and 'mouth'.

Forgiveness, therefore, is a natural
thing—it is 'like the heart' to forgive, for
human nature is naturally benevolent.

Ambition   Chih

We sometimes speak of ambitious people as
having their mind or heart set on their goal.
Since the Chinese make no distinction between the 'heart', and the 'mind' or 'inten-
tions', we find the 'heart' pictogram at the root
of the character for 'ambition'.

Above the 'heart' is the 'scholar', represented by the character for 'ten' or 'complete'.
Scholars who have set their heart on it complete their studies, and in so doing become
complete persons.

一
十
士
士
志
志
志

Love   Ai

The character for *ai*, the 'love' that one person
feels for another, suggests that although the
word is now used as freely in China as else-
where, love was once considered a highly
spiritual emotion. Some sages believed it to be
a form of giving that should be extended not
only to those closest to us, but to more distant
members of society as well.

In the center is the 'heart' pictogram.
Above and below 'heart' are the characters
for 'breath' and 'graceful movement'. Love,
therefore, can be seen as a kind of inspiration.
It breathes life into the heart, and brings grace
to the body.

Patience   Jên

There is a well-known Chinese saying—
"The character for patience has a knife over
the heart." In other words, it is unwise to
provoke a person's patience.

However, the truly patient heart is a firm
one. In the character for *jên*, the 'knife blade'
(a developed form of an early pictogram)
bears down on the 'heart', yet the heart perse-
veres and endures.

Jên can also be translated as 'tolerance';
the Chinese language makes no distinction
between this attribute and 'patience', for the
firm heart is also a tolerant one.

刁
刀
刃
刃
忍
忍
忍

Loyalty   Chung

The character for *chung*, meaning both 'loyalty' and 'patriotism', shows a 'heart' beneath
a pictogrammatic representation of an arrow
piercing a target through its 'center'. This
shows that loyalty—whether it is to country,
person, or principle—means having a cen-
tered heart. A heart that is in the center is a
heart in the right place.

However, a steadfast heart does not imply
blind loyalty. Confucius taught that the truly
loyal minister should openly criticize his ruler's
mistakes. "What is loyalty," said the sage, "if
it does not instruct its subject?"

忠

Wisdom   Chih

The character for 'wisdom' is a complex one
with a simple message. Above is the word
'knowledge' formed by a combination of 'oath'
on the left and the small, squared-off pictogram for 'mouth' or 'spoken' on the right:
what we swear to in words, we know to be
true. Below 'knowledge' is the character for
'sun'—like 'mouth', a squared-off abstraction
of an ancient pictogram.

Wisdom: the knowledge that spreads and
enlightens like the sun's rays, benefitting the
world at large.

63

Devotion　　　　　　　　　Hsin

To be utterly devoted to someone implies having supreme trust in that person. The spiritual devotee must abandon all doubts in order to unquestioningly follow the sage.

What kind of person can inspire this kind of devotion? The answer is contained in the character for *hsin*—the abbreviated form of the pictogram for 'human being' (known as the 'crooked person radical' because only one leg stands on the ground), beside the character for 'words' (a 'mouth' from which emanate sound waves).

Persons who stand by their word inspire devotion in others.

Sincerity   Ch'eng

'Words' emanating from the 'mouth', with 'perfection', produce the character for 'sincerity', an attribute considered foremost on the path to enlightenment.

"Sincerity is the Way of Heaven. The attainment of sincerity is the Way of men," says the *Chung Yung*, a classic work of Confucianism. *Ch'eng* is the perfection of self, but more important, as the perfection of others through its practice in human relationships.

Sincerity: perfection through the transformation of thought into words.

Harmony   Ho

According to the *Chung Yung*, "once *chung* and *ho* are established, heaven and earth maintain their proper positions, and all creatures are nourished."

Chung is the 'just rightness' of things, while *ho* is everything in proper proportion. The person with moderate emotions and desires can be satisfied, and so achieves a state of inner and interpersonal harmony. Since all parts of the universe mirror one another, harmony among people is mirrored in heaven and in nature. Therefore, the character for *ho* shows a 'mouth' next to 'grain' ripe and heavy enough to make it bend at the top.

Harmony: that time when all creatures will be nourished.

Sage   Sheng

In the character for 'sage', 'divine', and
'holy', the pictogrammatic 'mouth' is preceded by the image of an 'ear', above the
character for 'great' or 'artful'—a character
that derives from the word for 'far north', the
ultimate point.

This character shows that the sage is gifted
in the arts of listening and speaking. But the
listening comes first, because through listening
one gains an understanding of the universe.
Since the sage has found oneness with the
universe, which is eternal, he too is eternal
and therefore divine.

Happiness   Fu

Confucius said, "With coarse rice to eat, with only water to drink, and my bended arm for a pillow, I am happy." Absolute happiness, he contended, comes not from material things but from one's inner life.

Nevertheless, Confucius realized that happiness means different things to different people, and that for most in his day it meant an existence untroubled by the hunger that was endemic to the life of a serf. Indeed, the Chinese character for happiness, *fu*, is formed around the idea of a full stomach. It combines 'to fill'—made by joining a 'mouth', a cultivated 'field', and 'one' or 'united'—with 'heaven', the source of abundance.

72

Melancholy   Ch'ou

The 'heart', tongues of 'fire', and heavy-headed 'crops' signify 'melancholy', that bittersweet feeling which comes in the fall, and has been celebrated over the ages in Chinese painting, poetry, and song.

In the fall, when ripened crops are harvested and fire prepares the fields for next year's yield, the heart grows sad, just as it does in the autumn of life. Yet this sadness takes on a special flavor when one contemplates the eternal cycle of life and death, fullness and decay.

Glory Hua

In the early days of Chinese writing, the character for 'flower', *hua*, was a simple pictogram showing many blades of 'grass' on a stem. In time, 'flower' became a more complex character. But the original pictogram, and the word *hua*, were adopted to signify 'glory' and 'splendor'.

The Chinese combine this ancient character for *hua* with 'person' to signify 'the glorious people'—the people of China.

Courage   Ying

A 'person' with arms spread wide to signify 'adult', standing alone in a 'wide open space' thick with 'grass'—a wilderness—signifies 'courage' and 'heroism', for he does not fear this place where wild animals roam.

In Chinese thought, the hero courageously endures nature's hardships by harmonizing with his environment, as did the sage-kings of China who, in the mythical Golden Age, were tested in forests and on mountaintops, among lions and through storms.

Vigor   Chien

Chien is a complex character, and something of a riddle. It is made up of the ideas 'to establish', and 'person', perhaps referring to the strength and vitality of those who are able to establish themselves in the world.

The character for 'to establish' is, in itself, complicated, combining a clawlike 'hand' holding the stem of a 'writing stick' and two written 'lines' to make 'pen', with the lively strokes of 'to move on'—suggesting the importance of writing as a means to power and influence in ancient China.

健健健健

Honesty   Shih

The character for 'honesty', *shih*, goes back
to the early days of Chinese civilization, pro-
viding a fascinating insight into a culture that
focused itself entirely on the moral nature of
the 'superior man' or aristocrat.

In ancient China, shells were used as currency, and even today the word 'money' or
'cash' is represented by the pictogram depicting a 'cowrie shell'. Here, a string of 'ten
thousand' 'shells' or coins is placed under a
'roof'. The person who has a fortune must be
an aristocrat, by definition a 'superior' and
honest person.

Honor   Kuei

We 'honor' that which is worthy, or of high
worth—an idea implicit in the Chinese character *kuei*, literally a 'basket' of 'cowrie shell'
currency. In ancient times, only the wealthy
aristocracy was considered worthy of honor.
For this reason, *kuei* also signifies 'expensive'.

   As Chinese philosophy developed, so did
the concept of 'honor'. Confucius taught his
aristocratic students to set an example to the
masses by honoring all those with whom they
came into contact, regardless of their wealth.
In Taoism, honor became an inner quality
"more precious than the finest jade," yet concealed beneath humble garments.

84

貴

賢
貴
貴
貴

Revelation Shih

The character *shih* means 'revelation', 'heaven-sent', an 'omen', 'to manifest', and 'to proclaim'. It is a stylized form of an ancient pictogram that showed three vertical lines of power or light emanating from the two horizontal strokes representing 'heaven'—the upper world that presides over nature.

Revelation: that which is revealed by the gods above.

Propriety   Li

Combining a 'sacrificial vessel' alongside 'revelation' or 'heaven-sent', the character for 'propriety' shows us something of the history of this important concept in Chinese culture.

Originally *li* meant simply 'sacrifice', denoting observance of ceremonial ritual in order to interpret the will of heaven. Confucius enlarged the meaning of *li* to include correctness in dealings with others—for if his students were to become rulers, and treat people with respect, order would come to society.

88

Piety   Hsiao

The character for 'piety' describes the correct relationship between parent and child. Above is the 'old' person, or 'elder'—an ideogram combining 'person', 'hair', and 'change' to poignantly suggest the physical process of aging. Below the 'elder' is the 'child', from an ancient pictogrammatic stick drawing of a baby. The child defers to, supports, and is dedicated to the parent.

  This is the ideal of filial piety, a principle strongly promoted by Confucius, which remained central to Chinese culture for at least two thousand years.

Reverence　　　　　　Ch'ung

A 'revelation' or 'manifestation' under one's 'roof' produces the character for 'ancestor' or *tsung*, the vital link between a person and the very origin of his or her family. Worshipped and revered in Chinese culture since the dawn of civilization, ancestors are traditionally buried on the mountainsides as a sign of respect. Therefore, the character for 'reverence' places the 'ancestor' below the three peaks of a 'mountain', reminding us to revere those who came before.

Destiny   Ming

In Chinese thought, 'destiny' refers not so much to a predetermined path in life as to the fact of death, which is the destiny of all life and the law of nature.

Perhaps for this reason, the written word *ming* begins with a character meaning originally 'to agree'—a combination of 'person', 'one', and 'mouth'—and by extension 'mandate', and 'to close' both physically and figuratively. To this character is added a 'seal' or 'chop', also signifying an allotted 'time' or 'duration'. Thus, several ideas are at play. Our destiny, or allotted time, is sealed; and when the door closes on life it is by mandate of heaven.

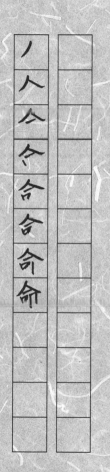